GOD, GOVERNMENT AND THE GOOD SAMARITAN

The Promise and the Peril of the President's Faith-Based Agenda

Joseph Loconte

The Heritage Foundation

Published by
The Heritage Foundation
214 Massachusetts Avenue, NE
Washington, DC 20002–4999
800-544-4843
www.heritage.org

Copyright © 2001 The Heritage Foundation

ISBN 0–89195–101–6

First edition 2001
Second printing 2002

Cover design by Mark Hurlburt
Cover image, "The Good Samaritan," a 19th century
woodcut by Julius Schnoor von Carolsfeld, first appeared
in *Das Buch der Bücher in Bilden.*

I do not know if all Americans have faith in their religion—for who can read the secrets of the heart?—but I am sure that they think it necessary for the maintenance of republican institutions.

—Alexis de Tocqueville

ACKNOWLEDGEMENTS

The author would like to thank Adam Meyerson for his great encouragement, clear thinking and patient editing, which—as always—vastly improved the manuscript. Special thanks as well to colleagues Matthew Spalding and Herb Berkowitz, who took time from busy schedules to offer very useful critiques.

INTRODUCTION

*P*resident George W. Bush's creation of a White House Office of Faith-Based and Community Initiatives has stirred an unprecedented national conversation about the role of faith in public life. The President clearly intends to elevate the importance of religion in alleviating social ills. His strategy includes tax policies to boost donations to religious charities, reductions in regulations that hinder their work, and federal funding to faith-based groups previously excluded from government support. It is an agenda aimed at reversing decades of hostility to social programs rooted in religious belief.

Most of the debate so far has focused on church-state questions raised by the President's plan. Liberals worry about religious influence in government, while some conservatives fear exactly the opposite. Both sides, however, are missing the real import of Bush's approach to religion and the public square. Not since Dwight D. Eisenhower has a president used the bully pulpit as aggressively to tout the importance of faith to democratic government. "Without God, there could be no American form of government," Eisenhower bluntly put it, "nor an American way of life."[1] Eisenhower viewed faith as a bulwark against Communism

---

1. Marty Marty, *Modern American Religion: Under God, Indivisible: 1941–1960,* Vol. 3 (Chicago: University of Chicago Press, 1996), p. 296.

abroad and corruption and materialism at home. It was at his urging that the words "under God" were added to the Pledge of Allegiance.[2]

President Bush seems no less persuaded that faith is required to keep the democratic machine up and running. "Americans are generous and strong and decent," he said at his inaugural, "not because we believe in ourselves but because we hold beliefs beyond ourselves." His entire initiative assumes that religion's ability to change lives is essential to the nation's welfare. "In every instance where my administration sees a responsibility to help people," Bush pledged during the presidential race, "we will look first to faith-based organizations, charities and community groups that have shown their ability to save and change lives."

America's war on terrorism must not blunt the urgency of the President's message. The nation's internal threats are real and deep: The breakdown of families and communities—and the moral commitments that make them possible—is ravaging civic life in America. And, once again, belief in God is the indispensable weapon.

If the President's rhetoric is taken seriously, no social problem would be immunized from the civilizing influence of religion. If he confronts the deepest flaws of the welfare state, he could help shift resources from failed secular programs toward those with a moral backbone. While liberals are willing to speak approvingly of the benefits of faith, they are unwilling to allow religious organizations to

---

2. Alan Ehrenhalt, *The Lost City* (New York: Basic Books, 1995), p. 223.

assume any of the social service functions controlled by government. If Bush pushes the logic of his own initiative, this is exactly the direction his reforms are headed.

There are great risks involved. The funding plan could simply morph into a more sanctimonious version of the Great Society. Churches, synagogues, and private charities might look first to Washington for support, sending civil society itself into a ditch from which it may never emerge. The administrative state would be strengthened, while Bush's "compassionate conservatism" would be neutralized. There are fears that government would corrupt the religious impulse by seducing and then secularizing the charitable work of the faithful. Like the biblical figure Esau, they would sell their spiritual birthright for the pottage of public subsidies.

NO MORE
NAKED PUBLIC SQUARE

*F*ears, however, are no excuse for fatalism. No administration in recent times has been so willing to treat the faith community as a partner among equals. The President's agenda is a work in progress, but several themes have emerged as his argument against a political culture indifferent to faith. If advanced with great energy—and great care—these themes could help restore religious conviction as the bedrock of civic and political life:

First, religious organizations must be allowed a larger public role in fighting social ills. Any honest look at existing social programs reveals a landscape mostly barren of religious markers. Social science researchers, who have done so much to shape the assumptions of the welfare state, have largely ignored issues of faith. Theda Skocpol, a professor of government at Harvard, admits that the academic literature on social welfare policy "has been so dominated by leftist secularists that it has written out of the record positive contributions from religiously inspired service to the poor."[3]

---

3.   Theda Skopcol, "Religion, Civil Society, and Social Provision in the U.S.," in *Who Will Provide? The Changing Role of Religion in American Social Welfare*, Mary Jo Bane, Brent Coffin, and Ronald Thiemann, eds. (Boulder, Colo.: Westview Press, 2000), p. 24.

Another source of indifference is the courts. From about the 1940s onward, Supreme Court rulings have marginalized faith from public institutions. In cases such as *Bowen v. Kendrick* (1988), the court has prohibited government money from going to groups considered "pervasively sectarian"—that is, overtly religious—regardless of their public function. The effect has been to keep religiously robust providers on the margins of social policy debates.

> THE PRESIDENT'S AGENDA IS IMPORTANT NOT BECAUSE IT PROMISES FEDERAL MONEY, BUT BECAUSE IT PROMOTES CIVIC TRUST BY RESPECTING THE RELIGIOUS BELIEFS AND INDEPENDENCE OF THE NATION'S GOOD SAMARITANS.

President Bush's White House Office of Faith-Based and Community Initiatives challenges this secular zeitgeist: "Starting now, the federal government is adopting a new attitude to honor and not restrict faith-based and community initiatives ... and to empower rather than ignore them."[4] This is the White House mantra on religion in public life. That Bush is serious is evident from the people he tapped to implement his plan.

John DiIulio, a professor of government and a leading researcher of church-based social services at the University

---

4. George W. Bush, "Rallying the Armies of Compassion," statement announcing the President's faith-based initiative, *www.whitehouse.gov/news/reports/faithbased.html.*

of Pennsylvania, took a leave of absence to head up the office. (He resigned in August 2001 to return to his duties in Philadelphia.) Don Eberly, founder of the National Fatherhood Initiative and a foremost thinker on civil society, serves as deputy director. Carl Esbeck, a law professor and former director of the Christian Legal Society, is at the Justice Department to scrutinize government regulations unfriendly to faith-based charities.

The White House plan is to use law, public policy, and the bully pulpit to extend the compassionate reach of churches and religious groups. Bush has floated several ideas: allow religious charites to compete for federal money on an equal footing with secular agencies; expand the charitable deduction to cover taxpayers who do not itemize on their tax returns; limit the liability of corporations that donate equipment and facilities to charitable groups; allow contributions from IRAs without penalty; and promote a charity tax credit, in which taxpayers could send a portion of their tax bill to poverty-fighting groups.

The Community Solutions Act (H.R. 7), introduced by J.C. Watts (R–OK), and passed by the House in July, includes some of the President's initiatives. Most important, the bill would make it easier for religious groups to receive federal funding for their social outreach—without sacrificing their religious mission. A Senate version of the bill (S. 592), introduced by Rick Santorum (R–PA), focuses on tax incentives to increase charitable giving. As of this writing, it is unclear how far the Senate will go in embracing the President's agenda.

Attention—and criticism—has settled on the funding plan. For decades, government has subsidized the mercy work of hospitals and international relief organizations; of drug-treatment facilities and homeless shelters; of religious agencies such as Lutheran Social Services, Catholic Charities, and Jewish Federations. From soup kitchens to summer-camp ministries, secular and religious charities use public money for their outreach. Precise figures are difficult to come by, but this "government-by-proxy" system—in the form of grants, vouchers, and health-care reimbursement—sends billions of dollars to nonprofit groups every year. Some of the nation's largest religious charities receive more than half their budgets from public sources.

HOSTILITY TO RELIGIOUSLY INFORMED VALUES, SO DEEPLY ENTRENCHED IN SOCIAL SERVICES, WILL NOT BE UPROOTED WITHOUT POLITICAL MUSCLE.

With the money, however, comes pressure to wipe clean all signs of faith commitment—from menorahs to mealtime prayers. A housing program funded by the Department of Housing and Urban Development (HUD), for example, requires that emergency shelters operate "in a manner free of religious influence." State and local rules appear to be much more onerous, with prohibitions against evangelism or the distribution of religious literature. Even the right to control hiring decisions can be negated by government fiat.

A conservative Congress challenged this regime by passing the "charitable choice" law in 1996 as part of welfare reform.[5] The law makes it illegal for federal grantors to exclude organizations from funding because of their religious beliefs. While public money cannot be used for religious activities, charitable groups accepting government aid need not renounce their spiritual identity. First, organizations maintain sole control over "the definition, development, practice and expression" of their religious mission. Government may not, for example, force them to remove religious literature or icons from their facilities or dictate the composition of their board of directors. Second, they retain the right to hire staff who share their religious values. The freedom of faith-based groups to make employment decisions based on religion, reinforced by the 1964 Civil Rights Act, is considered a constitutionally protected right.[6]

Though untested in the courts, four separate charitable choice measures were passed by Congress and signed into

---

5. The Personal Responsibility and Work Opportunity Reconciliation Act of 1996, H.R. 3734, 104th Congress, 2d Session, P.L. 104–193.

6. As Supreme Court Justice William Brennan has put it: "Determining that certain activities are in furtherance of an organization's religious mission, and that only those committed to that mission should conduct them, is thus a means by which a religious community defines itself. Solicitation for a church's ability to do so reflects the idea that furtherance of the autonomy of religious organizations often furthers individual religious freedom as well." From *Corporation of Presiding Bishop* v. *Amos*, 483 US 327, 342–343 (1987). See also Carl H. Esbeck, *The Regulation of Religious Organizations as Recipients of Governmental Assistance* (Washington, D.C.: The Center for Public Justice, 1996).

law by President Clinton. The law's provisions now govern roughly $20 billion in Temporary Assistance to Needy Families (TANF) money, community service block grants, and drug and alcohol treatment programs.[7] Bush wants to expand the scope of the protections to include social-service programs across the board. The House legislation would cover more than 80 federal programs worth about $53 billion a year, ranging from job training to domestic violence.

There are great risks involved with federal funding for religious groups, but they must not be allowed to obscure the real significance of charitable choice. The President's plan could make more money available to inner-city ministries previously shunned by government or overlooked by private donors. For children at risk of slipping into poverty or violence—the prime beneficiaries of church-based urban outreach—that's important.[8] But federal help probably would amount to a fraction of the roughly $74 billion

---

7. Congress first passed charitable choice legislation in 1996 as part of the Welfare Reform Act, affecting federal funds under the Temporary Assistance to Needy Families (TANF) program. It was extended to include the Community Services Block Grant (CSBG) program in 1998. It was extended twice in 2000 to include drug and alcohol treatment programs under the Substance Abuse and Mental Health Services Act (SAMHSA). According to figures from the Republican Study Committee, most of the funds affected by existing charitable choice law (about $16.5 billion) apply to the TANF program, and half of that goes out in cash payments to individuals.
8. Ram A. Cnaan, "Keeping Faith in the City: How 401 Urban Religious Congregations Serve Their Neediest Neighbors," University of Pennsylvania and Public/Private Ventures, CRRUCS Report 2000-1.

given by Americans each year to churches and religious charities.

Charitable choice is landmark legislation not because it opens up federal coffers to religious groups, but because it helps restore civic trust. It enshrines into public policy two basic ideas: that government must not discriminate against charitable organizations guided by their belief in God, and that these Good Samaritans should not be forced to give up their spiritual identity to collaborate with government.[9]

Hostility to religiously informed values, so deeply entrenched in social services, will not be uprooted without political muscle. A recent study by the Center for Public Justice, for example, revealed that most states are ignoring the charitable choice law. They often exclude faith-based organizations from their social-service system, while those included are obliged to keep religious belief in the closet. It is unclear how aggressively bureaucrats enforce regulations that hobble the work of private charities. To find out, Bush signed an executive order in January 2001 establishing offices in five of the largest federal agencies—Justice,

---

9.   The law merely follows the most recent Supreme Court decisions by insisting on the equal treatment of religious groups when public money is made generally available. Last year's 6–3 decision in *Mitchell* v. *Helms*, for example, held that government-funded computers could go to parochial schools, as long as the assistance was available to public and private secular schools. The majority ruled that government may fund faith-based organizations if the purpose is to achieve legitimate secular purposes—boosting literacy rates, for example—but not to advance religion. By allowing a Catholic school to receive government support, the Court effectively ended its previous ban on assistance to "pervasively sectarian" groups. Charitable choice, then, is the legislative cousin to the Court's emerging principle of non-discrimination.

Labor, Education, Health and Human Services, and Housing and Urban Development—to identify needless rules and regulations. The audits, completed in July, show that government favors large, bureaucratic agencies over faith-based community groups.[10] The report's findings are sure to put pressure on states to get in line with existing law.

> "THE PRESIDENT HAS MADE A CONVINCING CASE FOR THE CONSTRUCTIVE CONTRIBUTIONS FAITH-BASED GROUPS CAN MAKE IN MEETING REAL SOCIAL NEEDS."
>
> —*Democratic Senator Joseph Lieberman*

Already the initiative has created momentum for church and state to work together. Fifteen states have appointed government liaisons to broker agreements between ministers and social-service departments, while at least 120 mayors have done the same.[11] What is striking is that many of the emerging partnerships involve little or no government funds. In Sacramento, a group of 30 black Protestant and Latino Catholic churches are saying no to public money, yet mobilizing volunteers to support the city's Department of Human Assistance. The city now refers over 200 clients to the churches for help in job searches and preparation. Says Amy Sherman of the Hudson Institute: "While fami-

---

10. "Unlevel Playing Field," Report from the White House Office of Faith-Based and Community Initiatives, released August 16, 2001.
11. Laurie Goodstein, "States Steer Religious Charities Toward Aid," *The New York Times,* July 21, 2000.

lies affected by welfare reform may continue to need temporary, emergency assistance, they need much more the personal and practical support individual congregants can provide."[12]

Over the last several months, officials at corrections departments from Michigan, New Mexico, and Nebraska have called Prison Fellowship to learn how to involve congregations in the lives of offenders and ex-offenders. Says Prison Fellowship's Pat Nolan: "Bush has given government employees a clear signal that it is OK to include churches in their work."

In Chicago, several hundred congregations have gotten involved in the city's public schools to offer after-school programs and safe havens. "We do everything with the churches," says former superintendent Paul Vallas, "short of evangelizing." In Kansas City, Missouri, Urban Campus Ministries has expanded its summer reading program to reach 300 high-poverty school children. In Philadelphia, Mayor John Street has set up a municipal office to help negotiate agreements, and personally appealed to churches to "adopt" city schools. In less than six months, congregations—with administrative support from the city—have mobilized over 600 volunteers as tutors and mentors for at-risk youth, effectively doubling the size of the city's Big Brother/Big Sister program. Street calls these efforts "the last, best hope" for the needy.[13]

---

12. Amy Sherman, "The Growing Impact of Charitable Choice," The Center for Public Justice, March 2000, p. 19.
13. Judy Pasternak, "Philadelphia Mayor Relies on Faith to Deliver Services," *The Philadelphia Inquirer*, April 9, 2001.

At its best, the Bush initiative defies the assumption that faith carries no advantage over unbelief in healing social ills. At the very least, it's prodding policymakers to encourage the hands-on help of religious communities. Even many Democratic political leaders are abandoning their party's decades-old ambivalence toward religion.

During the 2000 presidential campaign—in his only major speech on religion during his eight years in office—Al Gore attacked the "hollow secularism" of intrusive government. Faith-based charities offer "another kind of help than the help given in government programs," Gore told the Salvation Army in Atlanta. "To the workers in these organizations, that client is not a number, but a child of God."[14] (Gore also endorsed charitable choice and pledged to expand it to other programs.) Sen. Zell Miller, a Democrat, has sent a dear-colleague letter urging support for the President's agenda. Sen. Evan Bayh chided fellow Democrats at a recent Democratic Leadership Council meeting for being perceived as anti-religious. "We have practically banished religious values and religious institutions from the public square," said Sen. Joseph Lieberman. "The President has made a convincing case for the constructive contributions faith-based groups can make in meeting real social needs."[15]

Second, the demoralized model of social services must give way to more humane assistance. The trademark of

---

14. Al Gore, speech delivered to the Salvation Army in Atlanta, May 24, 1999.
15. Remarks of Senator Joseph Lieberman, Pew Forum on Religion and Public Life, the National Press Club, March 1, 2001.

modern liberalism is what the President criticizes as "the soft bigotry of low expectations." It is an ethos that resists making any moral judgments about the poor, while pretending that high standards of behavior or achievement are unimportant.

The nation's major schools of social work have thoroughly imbibed this view. Professional social workers focus on their clients' circumstances, not their character, lifestyle, or the quality of their family relationships. Spiritual concerns are all but ignored.

It's easy to see where this thinking leads: Individuals come to be treated not as bearing a God-given dignity and capacity for self-improvement, but as wards of the welfare state. How else can we explain the massive growth in welfare spending over the last 35 years, even during periods of economic prosperity? "People are assets to be liberated rather than problems to be subsidized," says Marvin Olasky, author of *The Tragedy of American Compassion*. "People need to be treated as human beings made in God's image, not as animals to be fed, caged, and occasionally petted."[16]

As political philosopher Joel Schwartz notes, the view of the needy as helpless victims has deep roots. It represents a transformation in thinking about poor relief that began in the 19th century, in which environmental causes of poverty would trump most other considerations. The result, Schwartz says, is a "misguided egalitarian conviction that solidarity with the poor precludes our making distinctions

---

16. Marvin Olasky, *Renewing American Compassion* (New York: The Free Press, 1996), p. 33.

among them."[17] Whenever this idea took hold, it has lent credibility to massive federal investments in Great Society programs. Frances Fox Piven and Richard Cloward's *Regulating the Poor* and William Ryan's *Blaming the Victim* popularized the effort to demoralize government welfare policies. Gertrude Himmelfarb, history professor emeritus at the City University of New York, summarizes the problem this way: "We have so completely rejected any kind of moral principle that we have deliberately, systematically divorced poor relief from moral sanctions and incentives."[18]

The policy effects of this approach include homeless shelters with no work or educational requirements, after-school programs that teach "self esteem" but not virtue, family services that ignore marriage, and drug treatment that substitutes one addiction for another. Government spends roughly $150 billion a year on programs to support single-parent families, but spends only about $150 million on programs to reduce out-of-wedlock births.[19] The cultural consequences include more than a million women a year having children outside of marriage, more than 2 million people in state and federal prisons, and half of all high school seniors using illegal drugs.[20] Myron Magnet's semi-

---

17. Joel Schwartz, *Fighting Poverty With Virtue: Moral Reform and America's Urban Poor, 1825-2000* (Bloomington, Ind.: Indiana University Press, 2000), p. 134.
18. Gertrude Himmelfarb, "From Victorian Virtues to Modern Values," American Enterprise Institute, 1995.
19. Patrick Fagan, "Increasing Marriage and Discouraging Divorce," Heritage Foundation *Backgrounder* No. 1421, March 26, 2001.
20. See *The Index of Leading Cultural Indicators 2001* (Washington, D.C.: Empower America, 2001).

nal work, *The Dream and the Nightmare*, documents the utter failure of government approaches in the face of entrenched family breakdown and moral turpitude.

> SECULAR SCHEMES PRODUCE AFTER-SCHOOL PROGRAMS THAT TEACH "SELF ESTEEM" BUT NOT VIRTUE, FAMILY SERVICES THAT IGNORE MARRIAGE, AND DRUG TREATMENT THAT SUBSTITUTES ONE ADDICTION FOR ANOTHER.

Bush cites Magnet's work as a foundation for his compassionate conservatism, but he mostly avoids making a frontal attack on Great Society bromides about poverty. His criticism is more implicit. Consider the social ministries that get presidential attention: the Fishing School, an after-school program for poor children in Washington, D.C., run by a no-nonsense ex-cop; Grace Episcopal Church in Plainfield, New Jersey, where a musical youth group learns about personal responsibility while recording and marketing their own CDs; the Center for the Homeless in South Bend, Indiana, where families in drug treatment programs also enroll in a Great Books curriculum; or Tillie Bergin's Mission Arlington in Arlington, Texas, which provides food, medical care, and youth programs, mixed with Bible study and tough-love advice. Almost without fail, Bush chooses organizations that stress the importance of education, work, sexual responsibility, and faith. Compared with government-funded social services, these mom-and-pop ministries are quickly dismissed as a drop in the bucket; they could never supplant the welfare state. But that misses the point: Bush can use them to make an essentially moral argument against the permissive culture of government social policy. Indeed, not since Ronald Reagan has a president been so willing to employ a rhetoric of judgmentalism—the idea that certain behavior is just plain wrong and that government should stop subsidizing it.

Professor of government James Q. Wilson argues that a widespread reluctance to speak in moral terms "has amputated our public discourse at the knees."[21] Bush could help sew the legs back on. By connecting the charitable work of religious groups to personal responsibility, his speeches contain an unmistakable moral edge, without the stridency of a fiery televangelist. "A president can speak without apology for the values that defeat violence and help overcome poverty ... for abstinence and accountability and the power of faith," Bush said during the presidential race.[22]

In his inaugural address, Bush linked the soul-shaping work of religious groups to the public good: "Our public interest depends on private character, on civic duty and family bonds...." In announcing his faith-based agenda, he praised organizations that "treat people as moral individuals, with responsibilities and duties, not as wards or clients or dependents or numbers." At a commencement ceremony at Notre Dame, he argued that "much of today's poverty

---

21. James Q. Wilson, *The Moral Sense* (New York: The Free Press, 1993), p. xi.
22. George W. Bush, "The Duty of Hope," Indianapolis, Indiana, July 22, 1999.

has more to do with troubled lives than a troubled economy."[23] And at a Fourth of July celebration in Philadelphia, he said that the redeeming help of religious charities is "beyond the reach of government, and beyond the role of government."[24]

This theme clearly has resonance. Liberals seem more willing now to talk about accountability, even with issues as controversial as welfare or public school reform. The rise of the New Democrats signals a weariness with left-wing cant. Aside from Mario Cuomo, hardly anyone defends Big Government without a string of qualifiers. Bush is now primed to take his argument to the next step. While avoiding an anti-government tone, he can credibly expose a human-service regime that treats symptoms rather than causes and separates social outcomes from matters of the heart.

Third, black and Hispanic churches must be engaged in the task of urban renewal. The problems of urban America are ravaging minority populations. Out-of-wedlock births, incarceration rates, illiteracy, unemployment—all disproportionately affect blacks and Hispanics. Policymakers have largely turned a blind eye, however, to the best place for help in turning things around: the church. If religious leadership is brought on board, Bush's faith-based agenda could energize the social conservatism of blacks and Hispanics. It is the only way to repair the breakdown of fami-

---

23. George W. Bush, Remarks by the President in Commencement Address, University of Notre Dame, May 20, 2001.
24. George W. Bush, Remarks by the President in Independence Day Celebration, Independence Historic National Park, Philadelphia, Penn., July 2, 2001.

lies, schools, and communities that characterizes too many urban settings.

In a way no one predicted, the White House initiative has gotten the attention of a significant cast of minority leaders. "This puts the Republican Party and the President in direct contact with the lifeline of the African–American community," says the Rev. Herb Lusk of the Greater Exodus Baptist Church in Philadelphia. Rev. Eugene Rivers, a Democrat with close ties to John DiIulio, has called the initiative "one of the most promising opportunities black churches have had in the last 30 years."[25]

> THE PRESIDENT'S INITIATIVE IS GIVING VOICE TO A NEW GENERATION OF BLACK AND HISPANIC MINISTERS WHO ARE CALLING FOR MORAL REFORM WITHIN THEIR OWN COMMUNITIES.

That view seems to be gathering steam. According to a study of 1,236 congregations published in the 1999 *American Sociological Review*, nearly two-thirds of pastors from predominantly black churches said they would seek government funds for social-service projects. A survey released in April 2001 shows 81 percent support among African–Americans and Hispanics. The idea of greater cooperation between government and church-based charities has gotten high praise from the Rev. Walter Fauntroy, who marched

---

25. Mark O'Keefe, "Bush Charities Initiative Reaches Out to African-Americans," Newhouse News Service, 2001.

with Martin Luther King Jr.; Bishop T.D. Jakes, an internationally known preacher and leader of a megachurch in Dallas; the Rev. Floyd Flake, a former Democratic congressman and pastor of the 13,000-member church in Queens; and Bishop Charles Blake, a lifelong Democrat and pastor of an 18,000-member Church of God in Christ in West Los Angeles. Fifteen prominent ministers met with Bush earlier this year and pledged "uncompromising support" for his agenda.[26] Over 400 ministers and leaders of faith-based groups, mostly African–American, attended an all-day summit called by House and Senate Republican majority leaders, and praised the President's initiative.

While avoiding shallow partisanship, Bush can tap the conservative values of black and Hispanic churches to confront poverty and family disintegration. Surveys show that African–Americans are among the most religious and socially conservative groups in America. They tend to support traditional marriage, oppose abortion, and endorse school choice. Many have built extensive social-service ministries saturated in religious instruction.

Pastor Richard Salazar heads an association of over 100 Hispanic churches in Los Angeles that target high-risk kids. Every Saturday night, about 700 youth—most from poor families in bad neighborhoods—gather for fellowship and a Bible-based message. Bishop Jakes has founded the Metroplex Economic Development Corporation, a one-stop shopping approach that includes drug rehabilitation, adult education, and a referral program for ex-offenders.

---

26. Mike Allen and Thomas Edsall, "Black Religious Leaders Hear Bush's Call," *The Washington Post*, March 20, 2001, p. A6.

Says Jakes: "It won't be enough to introduce people to salvation if we don't change their lifestyles."

Tony Evans, pastor of Oak Cliff Bible Fellowship in Dallas, has developed a similar mix of Bible-based programs. "The process of meeting social needs through biblical solutions is not difficult or complex," he says. "It's available to the church if we just take the initiative to do it." Though conscious of the need to improve the social conditions of urban neighborhoods, these ministers mostly avoid the rhetoric of racism and victimization. Their watchwords: personal responsibility. Says Evans: "Our governing principle must be that poverty is best overcome by productivity."[27]

Even more liberal-minded ministers have designed initiatives that are models of economic empowerment through spiritual renewal. They are building affordable housing, starting private schools, running welfare-to-work programs. Bishop Charles Klingman oversees the Exodus Program, an employment agency spun off from his 3,000-member congregation in Cincinnati. "Christianity is what we live, breathe, and practice, but we don't thrust it upon people," he says. "We teach people how to go to work, pay their bills and become self-sufficient, instead of depending on an agency to bail them out of every crisis."[28]

---

27. Tony Evans, *America's Only Hope: Impacting Society in the 90s* (Chicago: Moody Press, 1990), p. 138.
28. Testimony before the Subcommittee on the Constitution of the Committee on the Judiciary, U.S. House of Representatives, April 24, 2001.

The ministries at Floyd Flake's Allen African Methodist Episcopal Cathedral are, in some ways, a throwback to those of 19th century moral reformers. Issues of personal and family responsibility are never off the radar screen. "Poverty is a reality for many individuals because they have not gotten their family relationships in order," says Flake. "It is our responsibility to reclaim the sanctity of marriage and the family. We have a duty to ourselves and especially to our children."[29] In addition to job training programs, the church sponsors 12 investment clubs for its members. Flake's church consistently helps the poor move from welfare to full-time employment.

> "POVERTY IS A REALITY FOR MANY INDIVIDUALS BECAUSE THEY HAVE NOT GOTTEN THEIR FAMILY RELATIONSHIPS IN ORDER."
> —*former Democratic Congressman Floyd Flake*

The moral dimension of the ministers' work tends to be ignored. No wonder. By pouring efforts into changing behavior as a prerequisite to economic mobility, they rankle economic planners. By insisting that religious belief is crucial to overcoming family breakdown, they mystify social workers. By stressing the importance of male leadership, they set feminists howling.

---

29. Floyd Flake and Donna Marie Williams, *The Way of the Bootstrapper: Nine Action Steps for Achieving Your Dreams* (San Francisco: HarperSanFrancisco, 1999), p. 152. See also Schwartz, *Fighting Poverty with Virtue:*, pp. 211–37.

All of this may put them out of step with black Democratic leadership, but not with rank-and-file churchgoers. According to opinion polls, most want to see the role of congregations in fighting poverty expanded. A dozen prominent African–American ministers have launched a National Center for Faith-Based Initiatives, a cross-denominational group to assist religious charities interested in applying for federal funds. Says John Perkins, a civil rights activist and 30-year veteran of church-based community development: "The alternatives to welfare and other social problems are clear, and the churches...prove that."[30]

Vernadette Broyles, a lawyer and welfare policy consultant, has been explaining the President's plan to enthusiastic crowds at meetings around the state of Georgia. Seventy-five percent of her audience is African–American, and they are growing increasingly confused about the lack of interest by the state's political establishment. "They will come to this crisis point," Broyles says. "More and more pastors are learning about this and will be demanding action from the state."

They already are. The Interdenominational Theological Center in Atlanta, home to the nation's largest consortium of black seminaries, recently held a conference to debate the initiative. Gerald Durley, former president of the Concerned Black Clergy in Atlanta, a left-wing association of Christians and Muslims, hopes to pressure the governor to push a faith-based initiative statewide. Manning Marable, director of African–American Studies at Columbia Univer-

---

30. John Perkins and Jo Kadlecek, *Resurrecting Hope* (Ventura, Calif.: Regal Books, 1995), p. 24.

sity, calls the mounting church support for the Bush plan "an end-run around these elites."[31] To some that's mere bluster, but clearly a debate has been joined within the African–American community that would have been unthinkable just a few years ago.

The need now is to take both the resources—and the limitations—of minority churches seriously. The African–American Christian tradition alone claims about 65,000 congregations and 20 million members. There are scores of independent black churches and no less than nine certified programs operated by seminaries to train members for the ministry. A 1990 survey of 2,100 congregations found that 71 percent engaged in community outreach.[32] Yet despite their near ubiquitous presence in the inner city, African–American churches struggle to keep their doors open, pay their ministers, and attract men to church life.

Political leadership has ignored the problem: Since the civil rights movement of the 1960s, black congregations have been enlisted for liberal political causes, not for community social action. Yale law professor Stephen Carter says that "the fortunes of the black clergy's leadership ... have become so bound up with the fortunes of the Democratic Party that it is no longer possible for the leaders to press ideas that their religious understanding of the world might demand."[33]

---

31. John Leland, "Some Black Pastors See New Aid Under Bush," *The Washington Post*, February 2, 2001.

32. John DiIulio, "Supporting Black Churches," *Brookings Review*, Spring 1999, p. 43. DiIulio cites a survey by Eric Lincoln and Lawrence Mamiya in their 1990 *The Black Church in the African-American Experience*.

The Bush initiative is giving voice to a new generation of black and Hispanic ministers who are calling for moral reform within their communities—for mothers to stop abusing drugs, for absentee fathers to claim paternity, for the unemployed to make themselves employable. If conservatives awaken to the opportunity, they could help accomplish a task left undone by Great Society programs: help marshal the moral and religious energy of minority congregations to combat poverty and family breakdown in urban America. "They're giving an ear to our community through the pastors," says Willie Brooks, pastor of the Bethesda Tabernacle Apostolic Church in San Diego, who attended the Washington summit. "I've never seen government taking such a concern for our community like they're doing now."[34]

33. Stephen Carter, *God's Name in Vain* (New York: Basic Books, 2000), p. 37.
34. Elizabeth Becker, "Republicans Hold Forum With Blacks in Clergy," *The New York Times*, April 26, 2001.

THE RISKS OF CHURCH-STATE AGREEMENTS

*T*hough much of the opposition to the President's initiative carries a shrill partisan note, there are concerns that shouldn't be dismissed out of hand. The first, coming mostly from secular liberals, is constitutional: *There is a fear that government support for religious groups amounts to the unlawful establishment of religion.*

Faith-based legislation pending in Congress is based on the 1996 charitable choice law. That law balances the two provisions on religion in the First Amendment—known as the "establishment" and "free exercise" clauses—to make federal money available to religious organizations helping the poor. Under the legislation, no government funds can be used for religious instruction, worship services, or proselytizing. If such activities are offered, they must be privately supported and segregated from the secular aspects of the program. Congregations are advised to set up separate nonprofits for their social outreach, while religious charities must create different budgets for the secular and religious parts of their programs, subject to government audits.

The problem is not that the law lacks clarity. The challenge is to follow the law without choking groups in bureaucracy.

It's true that many organizations have poor accounting systems or lack fiscal discipline; they will be tempted to commingle public and private funds. Others will have trouble untangling the spiritual from the secular parts of their programs, as it won't always be clear where social assistance ends and religious instruction begins. Nevertheless, charitable choice anticipates most of the scenarios that could rankle church-state watchdogs. Is Bible-reading as part of a literacy program, for example, permissible? Yes, if it's well-designed. Can government-paid counselors lead worship services? Not on program time.

Some groups are so "conversion-centered" that their religious objectives seem indistinguishable from any public secular goal. Can a drug treatment program get government grants if its recovery strategy is all about religious commitment? It shouldn't try. Most everyone agrees that taxpayers should not be forced to subsidize the evangelistic mission of religious organizations. There are ways to support these programs, but direct government grants are too problematic.

For opposite reasons, however, critics on the left and right have muddied the debate by holding out these programs as the litmus test for the President's agenda. Some opponents use a fear of "proselytizing" to justify discrimination against all religious providers. Some supporters talk as though the only successful programs are those with an altar call. But the variety of faith-based approaches is much richer and more diverse.

Critics also worry about coercion—the possibility that vulnerable people will be railroaded into religious programs. Go back to the law: Faith-based groups must offer help on a non-discriminatory basis. They may not require that people participate in religious activities. If someone objects to the religious character of a program, government must provide an alternative "within a reasonable period of time." Under these rules—all embodied in legislation now before Congress—how would anyone's religious liberty be compromised?

Fearmongers call Bush's faith-based initiative a "recipe for sectarianism" and a "radical assault" on the First Amendment. A study of church-state partnerships by the Hudson Institute's Amy Sherman, however, discovered only two cases where recipients joined a religious program and became uncomfortable with its message. The solution: They found a secular program down the street.[35] In fact, families struggling to survive in poor, dangerous neighborhoods tend to welcome help from religious organizations. Says Robert Woodson, president of the National Center for Neighborhood Enterprise: "When you talk to people who have lost a child to suicide, prison, or drug addiction, they have a different perspective."[36]

Carl Esbeck, who helped draft the original charitable choice legislation, argues that the ability to get help from a faith-based organization "is every bit an exercise of religious freedom as is the right not to be served by a religious provider."[37] In the five years since charitable choice was

35. Sherman, "The Growing Impact of Charitable Choice."
36. Robert L. Woodson, Sr., "Barriers to Faith-Based and Community Initiatives," Recommendations of the National Center for Neighborhood Enterprise, Washington, D.C.
37. Carl Esbeck, Testimony Before the Senate Judiciary Committee on Sec. 701 (Charitable Choice) of S. 304 Drug Abuse Education, Prevention, and Treatment Act of 2001, May 1, 2001.

first implemented, hundreds of new partnerships have emerged between state governments and religious organizations. Despite the best efforts of liberal groups such as Americans United for the Separation of Church and State, no court cases have challenged the constitutionality of the law. So where's the theocracy?

Another criticism is that government funding and oversight will seduce and corrupt religious programs. Richard Land, president of the Ethics and Religious Liberty Commission of the Southern Baptist Convention, says he "wouldn't touch the money with the proverbial ten-foot pole." Michael Horowitz of the Hudson Institute warns that secular nonprofits have become dependent on federal funds for their survival—and now wear the garb of "Beltway" lobbyists to protect their subsidies. "It would be catastrophic if churches developed a similar dependency on government," he says.[38]

The dangers are real. As my own research suggests, charities that chase public money easily fall victim to "mission creep," in which they drift away from their original priorities to offer whatever services government happens to be funding.[39] If they become too dependent on public support, they could be perceived as a government agency and lose their volunteer, community-based spirit.

The deeper worry is that groups with a strong religious mission ultimately will be forced to compromise their faith

---

38. Michael Horowitz, "Subsidies May Cost Churches Their Souls," *The Wall Street Journal*, December 16, 1999.

39. See Joe Loconte, *Seducing the Samaritan: How Government Contracts Are Reshaping Social Services* (Boston: the Pioneer Institute, 1997), pp. 33–54.

in order to comply with the law. There is no question that the pressure to define and segregate a program's religious components will be greatest when direct government grants are involved. Staff paid with public dollars, for example, can't simply function as ministers in plainclothes. Under most versions of the faith-based legislation enacted since 1996, individuals receiving assistance must be allowed to opt out of activities such as religious instruction or evangelism. Allowing people to stay in a program while avoiding some or all of its religious components, however, could undermine the integrity of faith-based charities. Is that the same as secularization? Many would say yes; they ought not to get involved with public funding at this level.

Nevertheless, guarding the independence of religious charities may have less to do with their funding source than with their faith commitments. Boston University's Charles Glenn, after surveying scores of religious schools and charities, concluded that they can work successfully with government if they have a committed staff, a clear sense of mission, and a board of advisors who act as sentries to protect it. Without that, they face the more subtle danger of self-betrayal, what Glenn simply calls "the loss of nerve."[40]

Ed Morgan, president of New York City's Bowery Mission, a 122-year-old Christian program for homeless men with substance abuse problems, has seen it happen before. Nevertheless, when the city offered in 1994 to help Morgan set up a separate Transition Center for men on the city's

---

40. Charles L. Glenn, *The Ambiguous Embrace: Government and Faith-Based Schools and Social Agencies* (Princeton: Princeton University Press, 2000), p. 241.

welfare rolls, he agreed. From the beginning, he vowed that if city officials pressured the Bowery Mission to do anything that violated its spiritual mission, he would walk away.

What part does faith play? A quiet one. Bibles, bought with private money, are provided only if requested. Weekly Bible studies, run by volunteers, are made available but attendance is not required. A 12-step recovery class might stir a spiritual discussion. And yet the program—fully funded by the city of New York—is ranked the most effective in helping homeless men off government assistance. "We found the key to accepting public funds is to design a separate, custom program, which balances public funding requirements and the fulfillment of our focused mission statement," Morgan says.[41]

The lesson: Faith-based groups can learn to negotiate government support, keep their spiritual bearings, and respect the First Amendment. However, public money can also lead to dependence and pressures to segment religious from non-religious activities. Many groups will rightly decide they are better off without it.

A final criticism of the Bush initiative is that it ultimately will reinforce—rather than challenge—the central assumptions of the Great Society. Much of what is wrong with the welfare system is its sheer size. A few years ago Catholic Charities did a taxonomy of publicly funded

41. Edward Morgan, "Building a Consensus on Public Funding," *Christian Management Report*, May/June 2001. See also Joseph Loconte, "Dual Mission," *The Wall Street Journal*, February 2, 2001.

social services in New York City. Daycare, after-school programs, refugee resettlement, homeless shelters, drug treatment, food banks—they stopped counting at 227.[42] In 1999, federal and state governments devoted over $430 billion to welfare and social services, with huge gaps in accountability and lackluster results.[43] How could adding a relative handful of faith-based programs upset this blob?

Most Americans are unaware that there are over 325,000 churches, synagogues, and mosques in America, most of which have at least one program for the poor. Add to that thousands of religious nonprofits engaged in social outreach. Ron Sider, president of Evangelicals for Social Action, points to a study of Los Angeles neighborhoods that found an average of 35 congregations and 12.5 religious nonprofits per square mile. That's more than all the gasoline stations, liquor stores, and supermarkets in these neighborhoods combined.[44] "Especially in inner-city neighborhoods where almost every other institution has failed or disappeared," Sider says, "the very presence of religious congregations almost everywhere is an enormous strength."[45]

---

42. Joseph Loconte, "The Anxious Samaritan: Charitable Choice and the Mission of Catholic Charities," The Center for Public Justice, May 2000, p. 11.

43. Robert Rector, "Implementing Welfare Reform and Restoring Marriage," in Stuart M. Butler and Kim R. Holmes, eds., *Priorities for the President* (Washington D.C.: The Heritage Foundation, 2001), pp. 71–96.

44. Ron Sider, "Revisiting Mt. Carmel Through Charitable Choice," *Christianity Today*, June 11, 2001, p. 86.

45. *Ibid.*

Recent studies by Ram Cnaan of the University of Pennsylvania and Carl Dudley and David Roozen of Hartford Seminary suggest that over 85 percent of churches offer desperately needed social services, attacking problems ranging from juvenile delinquency to drug addiction. According to Cnaan's study of 401 congregations in Philadelphia, the annual value of the services offered—including staff salaries, volunteer hours, and material assistance—amounted to $103,000 per church.

Where did it go? "It is widely assumed that urban congregations develop programs mainly to assist their own members, and that their programs are limited to those who belong to their church, synagogue, mosque, or community of faith," says Cnaan. "Wrong." The typical person helped is an at-risk child whose family does not attend the church.[46]

Despite these vast human and financial resources, there is little talk about how their capacity to assume more responsibility for the poor might be greatly expanded. "It is worth debating to what extent faith-based organizations replace government activities," says *Washington Post* columnist E.J. Dionne, "and to what extent they supplement them."[47] Most liberals, however, tremble at this prospect because of how it might upset the demoralized status quo. "There is a real danger," complains the *New Republic*,

---

46. Ram Cnaan, "Keeping the Faith in the City: How 401 Urban Religious Congregations Serve Their Neediest Neighbors."
47. E.J. Dionne, "Religion's Third Renegotiation with the Public Square," in *Religion and the Public Square in the 21st Century*, Ryan Streeter, ed. (Indianapolis, Ind.: The Hudson Institute, 2001, p. 29.

"that such support may come at the expense of secular and government alternatives."[48] That is exactly the point: A larger role for faith-based poverty-fighters means a smaller role for the administrative state.

> BUSH MUST DO MORE THAN INVITE RELIGIOUS CHARITIES INTO THE GOVERN-MENT SYSTEM; HE MUST BE WILLING TO REFORM THAT SYSTEM AT ITS CORE.

There is little sign, however, that the White House or Congress would scale back sacred-cow social programs. Bush boasts his budget will increase federal funding for welfare and poverty programs by eight percent. He intends to expand Bill Clinton's dubious AmeriCorps. He's pledged to set up a Compassion Capital Fund, which would match federal money with private contributions to community-based charities. If put into the hands of mayors to administer, expect politicization, set-asides, and graft.

Which prompts a question: What message does Washington send to the heroes of civil society when the bellwether of civic approval is a government contract to do its bidding? Bush recently visited Habitat for Humanity, for example, and pledged to triple its federal support. But the faith-based charity built its reputation for providing affordable housing on its *volunteers*. Habitat's most famous advocate, Jimmy Carter, never suggested it become a gov-

---

48. Benjamin Soskis, "Act of Faith: What Religion Cannot Do," *The New Republic*, February 26, 2001, p. 23.

ernment program. On the contrary, Habitat proved its worth to the community by getting results and attracting private money and manpower.

The President flexed enough political muscle to win an historic tax cut, a good way to help slow the growth of government. As *The New York Times* lamented the day after its passage, "some of the other things [Americans] want out of Congress cannot get enacted because of what was signed into law yesterday."[49] Nevertheless, Bush has been careful—too careful—to emphasize that government must occupy the central place in solving social problems. While Don Eberly at the White House Office of Faith-Based and Community Initiatives warns against trying to orchestrate social renewal from Washington—"that would be like the trees moving the wind"—others are more optimistic about revitalizing government's social safety net. That debate aside, there has been much more talk of supplementing federal programs than replacing bad ones with private, faith-based alternatives. This strategy could finally derail the effort to elevate the role of faith in addressing social problems.

The President's attention to religious charities is both remarkable and refreshing. The sad, neglected truth, however, is that not all charities are equal; many have become morally neutered clones of government programs. They provide cheaper child care, for example, but offer little more than lunch and unstructured play time. They give homeless men a sandwich and a place to sleep, but watch

---

49. "The Presidential Tax-Cut Moment," *The New York Times*, June 8, 2001, p. A26.

them get drunk or do drugs outside the shelter walls. They give unwed teen mothers contraceptives instead of tough talk about promiscuity. The administration would do well to recall the most potent argument for revolutionary welfare reform in the mid-1990s: The problem was not that welfare was costing too much, but that it was too stingy with the kind of help that offers hope and moral uplift to impoverished families.[50] Much government-funded charity is in the same leaky boat.

Repairing the vessel is a monumental task. Bush could begin by challenging the premises about government that nurture statist dreams, retard civil society, and dampen its most dynamic players—the communities of faith. The President must do more than invite religious charities into government's social-service system; he must also be willing to reform that system at its core.

---

50. See Marvin Olasky, *The Tragedy of American Compassion* (Washington, D.C.: Regnery Publishing, Inc., 1992).

LESSONS IN FAITH AND PHILANTHROPY

No one argues that the poor will be taken care of by a booming economy and private philanthropy alone. The problem is that too much faith is placed in Washington planners over the compassionate impulses of ordinary Americans. Given its historic role in American reform movements—abolition, the creation of public schools, women's suffrage, child labor laws—philanthropic action must lie at the heart of any effort to help the needy. And at the heart of philanthropy of this kind is faith. Religious values are among the strongest impulses for giving, while religious organizations are the favorite recipients of giving.

Until the early part of the 20th century, people of faith—working through churches, synagogues, associations, fraternal organizations, foundations—were the most reliable source of support to the down and out. They also were some of the fiercest critics of social evils, paving the way to great moral and political reforms. "If you read history," wrote C.S. Lewis, "you will find that the Christians who did most for the present world were just those who thought most of the next."[51] The real measure of the success of

---

51. C.S. Lewis, *Mere Christianity* (New York, N.Y.: Macmillan Publishing Co., Inc., 1979), p. 118.

Bush's initiative will not be in federal dollars to religious charities; it will be whether he helps revitalize, in the popular imagination and in government policy, the importance of religion to national renewal.

> "IF YOU READ HISTORY, YOU WILL FIND THAT THE CHRISTIANS WHO DID MOST FOR THE PRESENT WORLD WERE JUST THOSE WHO THOUGHT MOST OF THE NEXT."
> —*C.S. Lewis*

Who remembers, for example, that it was evangelical businessmen Arthur and Lewis Tappan who in the 1830s launched the American Anti-Slavery Society, the most important organization dedicated to abolition? Indeed, for decades the battle against slavery was led almost exclusively by religiously motivated dissenters. Likewise, when the U.S. government decided to forcibly remove Cherokee Indians from their native land in Georgia, who stood in the way? Christian missionaries. Petitions flooded Congress, while ministers were harassed and jailed. "The Cherokees are human beings," argued Jeremiah Evarts, "endowed by their Creator with the same natural rights as other men."[52]

It was the same for nearly every important social movement of the 19th century. Frances Willard, a devout Methodist, led the Women's Christian Temperance Union into picking up the mantle for labor unions and for women's

---

52. John G. West, Jr., *The Politics of Revelation and Reason* (Lawrence, Kan.: University Press of Kansas, 1996), p. 177.

right to vote. In the 1860s, faced with perhaps 60,000 Irish children wandering in packs around New York City, philanthropist Levi Silliman Ives founded the Catholic Protectory. Ives rented housing for boys and girls on 86th Street. They would move to a 114-acre site in the Bronx that over the years would shelter over 100,000 children. The kids got more than a safe place to sleep: "Every child committed to this institution will be thoroughly trained in the faith and morality of the Gospel as revealed and entrusted to the Catholic Church."[53] The Protectory was the forerunner for Boys Town, today an acclaimed residential approach to helping severely troubled kids.

In the 1880s, as hundreds of thousands of Jewish immigrants began pouring into New York City, financier Jacob Henry and social worker Lillian Wald founded two institutions—the Visiting Nurse Service and the Henry Street Settlement—that still minister to the people of New York. The Young Men's Christian Association (commonly known as the YMCA), backed by the philanthropy of wealthy church members, aimed to ease poverty by promoting "the welfare of the whole man—body, soul and spirit."[54] Joined by the YWCA, they functioned practically as a Protestant denomination. Job training was offered right along with Bible classes, while gymnasiums doubled as worship halls.[55] By 1900 there were nearly 1,500 local YMCA chapters with 250,000 members.

---

53. William Stern, "Once We Knew How to Rescue Poor Kids," in *What Makes Charity Work: A Century of Public and Private Philanthropy*, Myron Magnet, ed. (Chicago, Ill.: Ivan R. Dee, 2000), p. 32–40.

54. Olasky, *The Tragedy of American Compassion*, p. 130.

The Salvation Army, imported from Britain in 1880, brought its philosophy of "soup, soap and salvation" to some of the most destitute areas of the country. Within 20 years the group had spawned over 900 chapters, which combined shelters, stores, and workshops. Its employment bureaus were placing about 4,800 people a month.[56] Food, shelter, medical assistance, vocational training, prison ministry, legal aid for the poor, the provision of cheap coal in the winter—by offering these and other services, the Salvation Army soon became the most comprehensive Christian outreach to the cities.[57]

Historian Leo Trachtenberg calls these efforts "an object lesson in effective philanthropy that uplifts the poor instead of making them dependent."[58] Contemporary philanthropists could use a few lessons in the wise art of giving. In the past, notes Gertrude Himmelfarb, "the emphasis on the moral function of charity ... gave even secular philanthropies a quasi-religious character."[59] Not anymore. Most of the big foundations that fund social services—Ford, Mott,

---

55. Sydney Ahlstrom, *A Religious History of the American People,* Vol. 2 (Garden City, N.Y.: Double day and Company, Inc., 1975), p. 200.

56. Olasky, *The Tragedy of American Compassion,* p. 131.

57. Mark Noll, *A History of Christianity in the United States and Canada,* (Grand Rapids, Mich.: William B. Eerdmans Publishing Company, 1992), p. 304.

58. Leo Trachtenberg, "Philanthropy That Worked," in *What Makes Charity Work,* p. 69.

59. Gertrude Himmelfarb, "The Past and Future of Philanthropy," *Giving Better, Giving Smarter: Working Papers of the National Commission on Philanthropy and Civic Renewal,* John Barry and Bruno Manno, eds. (Washington, D.C.: National Commission on Philanthropy and Civic Renewal, 1997), p. 16.

Carnegie—follow the government model. They prize approaches that avoid making value judgments or challenge destructive behavior.

The problem is endemic. According to the Capital Research Center, six of the 10 largest corporate givers in America "ban or restrict" donations to religious charities, regardless of their track record.[60] Leslie Lenkowsky, professor of philanthropic studies at Indiana University, says it will be very difficult to undo the "profound wariness toward religious charities that one finds among the heirs, trustees, and professional staffers who now dominate the philanthropic world."[61] That's putting it gently. According to the General Motors Foundation policy, corporate contributions "generally are not provided to religious organizations."[62] In 1999, the leading 1,000 foundations sent just 2.3 percent of their grant dollars to religion.[63] Says Valerie Richardson, contributing editor of *Philanthropy:* "It may be easier for a camel to squeeze through the eye of a needle than to convince some foundations to open their grantmaking to church-run organizations."[64]

60. William Kristol, "Ya Gotta Believe," *The Weekly Standard*, March 26, 2001.
61. Leslie Lenkowsky, "Funding the Faithful: Why Bush Is Right," *Commentary*, June 2001, p. 21.
62. Jim VandeHei, "Bush Turns to Corporations to Help Fund Faith-Based Plan," *The Wall Street Journal*, May 24, 2001.
63. Valerie Richardson, "The Future of the Faith-Based Initiative," *Philanthropy,* May/June 2001, p. 10.
64. *Ibid.*

THE ROAD TO RENEWAL

*U*nder these circumstances, how can private philanthropy again become a catalyst for great social reform? And how can religious belief function as the engine that drives philanthropic endeavor? "The challenge before us now," says Don Eberly, "is to add to our determination to build down bad government an equal commitment to build up the good society."[65] Himmelfarb argues that a healthy civil society depends on healthy government—that is, a government with judicious laws and real limits on its power. While it's easy to overstate what government can do to reinvigorate philanthropy, federal policy can support and help instigate important cultural change.

First, the federal government must promote research to evaluate the effectiveness of secular and religious programs. Researchers haven't paid much attention to the "faith factor" in social policy. A recent evaluation of over 400 studies of juvenile delinquency, for example, found that barely 10 percent even took religious belief into account.[66] There are, in fact, few independent, credible studies of the efficacy of religious programs. What differ-

---

65. Don Eberly, "Compassionate Conservatism: Voluntary Associations and the Remoralization of America," *The Civil Society Project*, Vol. 2000, No. 1, p. 3.
66. Byron Johnson and David Larson, "Religion: The Forgotten Factor in Delinquency Research," prepared for The Manhattan Institute, November 13, 1998.

ence does faith make in a drug-treatment regimen such as Teen Challenge? Are religious programs really more effective than secular ones? We don't know.

The best social-science research, however, suggests a strong link between involvement in religious institutions and positive social outcomes. Dozens of empirically grounded studies show that where religious institutions thrive, predatory street crime is less severe.[67] Using data from the National Youth Survey, researchers Byron Johnson at the University of Pennsylvania and David Larson at Duke University Medical School found that religious belief has a "consistent direct effect on delinquency, independent of the effects of all the other variables controlled."[68] In other words, though we don't know exactly what role it plays when young men leave gangs or get off drugs, involvement in religion seems to be decisive.

A growing number of government officials—from wardens to welfare officers, from police to public-school principals—need little convincing. A church-based fatherhood program for court-involved men in Boston, for example, has become a favorite among judges and probation officers in the state. "I've been in law enforcement for 30 years," says Milton Britton, former chief probation officer who pushed the program in Massachusetts. "If you take out the church, the moral and spiritual thing, it ain't gonna

---

67. John DiIulio, "Building Spiritual Capital: How Religious Congregations Cut Crime and Enhance Community Well-Being," *Religion in American Life Briefing*, The Manhattan Institute, October 5, 1995.
68. Johnson and Larson, "Religion: The Forgotten Factor in Delinquency Research," p. 29.

work."[69] Visits to religious charities routinely uncover examples of people utterly transformed through the faith and friendship made available in these programs—homeless men who find good-paying jobs and move into their own apartments, felony offenders who gladly make restitution to their victims, prostitutes who kick their drug habits and get off the streets.

Are these groups doing a better job than government? We lack the data to say for certain. But if similar "prodigal son" stories were regularly generated by social service bureaucrats, one would expect to see a news release or two. Indeed, according to a recent White House report, virtually none of the big nonprofit groups favored by government funders for years have undergone a single systematic evaluation of performance.[70]

Mark Chaves, professor of sociology at the University of Arizona, denounces claims of the potency of faith-based programs as "completely without empirical basis."[71] To admit religious groups might be more adept than government at helping the poor is, of course, to concede the moral hollowness of secular schemes. And liberals are in no mood for confession: We now regularly hear left-wing ministers insist that faith commitment can't be counted on to treat social maladies. The University of Pennsylvania's John DiIulio, however, disagrees: "We already know more of a scientific nature about the extent and efficacy of these

---

69. Joseph Loconte, "The Bully and the Pulpit," *Policy Review*, November-December 1998.
70. John J. DiIulio Jr., "Unlevel Playing Field," *The Wall Street Journal*, August 16, 2001.
71. Benjamin Soskis, "Act of Faith: What Religion Cannot Do."

programs than the architects of the Great Society did when they launched their big-government initiatives in the 1960s."[72]

The long term need is for hard social-science data on religious as well as secular programs. Rigorous, longitudinal studies, however, take time. Meanwhile, Congress should promote a massive effort at basic evaluation research. Faith-based groups that hope to collaborate with government must learn to take stock of themselves—by defining their mission and objectives, keeping track of the people they serve, and developing yardsticks for measuring success. My colleague, research fellow Patrick Fagan, has launched a three-year project to help prepare faith-based groups interested in evaluating their programs. "Good intentions, even good faith-based intentions, are not the answer," Fagan says. "The public policy debate will demand that faith-based organizations deliver what they say they can."

Critics will complain this is descriptive, not scientific research. That's shortsighted. Even basic evaluation data are lacking for many government-funded services. As the debate over improving public schools makes clear, entrenched interests display a chronic lack of interest in learning from what works. Descriptive research helps policymakers—and potential donors—identify best practices. There are good reasons to suspect that some of the most effective approaches are rooted in faith commitment. Let's find out. Some private national organizations—such as the

---

72. John J. DiIulio Jr., "Know Us By Our Works," *The Wall Street Journal*, February 14, 2001.

Boy Scouts of America, Big Brothers/Big Sisters, and Goodwill Industries—already are moving in this direction. As more nonprofits, secular and religious, do the same, expect new buzzwords in social policy: accountability and effectiveness.

Second, conservatives fearful of government support for charities should put their money where their mouths are. There are legitimate worries when government subsidizes religious entities. Many swear off public funds altogether, and their hesitancy should be seen as a sign of the relative strength of religion in America—a strong commitment to protecting the independence of church and state. But that does not relieve religious organizations of their civic responsibilities. They can still work constructively with government without being on the public dole. They can team up with business entrepreneurs to tackle common problems.

Virgil Gulker, executive director of the Michigan-based Kids Hope USA, has launched perhaps the most carefully designed partnership between churches and public schools in the country. With permission from parents and school officials, congregations send volunteers into elementary classrooms to tutor and befriend at-risk kids. The methodology is disarmingly simple: give children at least an hour a week of unconditional love and support. "We have a growing number of kids who exhibit emotional and social needs that the teacher alone simply cannot meet. And until those needs are met, it is impossible for the child to learn," Gulker says. "I want the church to be an equal and exemplary partner with the schools in loving and nurturing children." Kids Hope—sustained by private money and volunteers—now deploys over 2,000 mentors in 157 schools across 24 states, with not a lawsuit in sight.

Two years ago Ted Forstmann, senior partner in a private investment firm, joined with WalMart heir John Walton to establish a private scholarship fund for children trapped in dead-end public schools. Their national lottery made 40,000 scholarships available to poor families, for use in private secular or religious schools. Applications arrived from 1.25 million children from all 50 states, sending shock waves through the education establishment. "Parents will never find what they seek unless we radically expand choice and opportunity in education," Forstmann said. "This is a moment of moral reckoning."[73] The Robert Wood Johnson Foundation recently announced its largest-ever commitment of funds to its Faith in Action program. The foundation will target $100 million to faith-based groups helping the chronically ill, elderly, or disabled. Says Steven Schroeder, foundation president and CEO: "It represents our deep belief that faith-based volunteer efforts are an effective way to address the growing needs of people with serious chronic conditions."[74]

A rising tide of civic leaders is reaching the same conclusion. The Council of Leadership Foundations works in 23 cities to bring together faith-based groups, city officials, and business leaders to solve community problems. Local

---

73. Ted Forstmann, "School Choice, by Popular Demand," *The Wall Street Journal*, April 21, 1999.
74. News release, the Robert Wood Johnson Foundation, March 28, 2001.

leaders are identified, trained, and brought into collaborations that cross racial, religious, and economic lines. In Memphis, the foundation is mobilizing congregations in gang outreach; in Minneapolis, there's a Center for Fathering to serve inner-city kids; in Fresno, it has a job coaching program; and in Pittsburgh there's a community storehouse to help over 175 religious groups serving the poor. Public-private ventures are also being run through the Christian Community Development Corporation, an association of over 400 partnerships to renew poor communities in roughly 100 cities. Led by a cadre of urban missionaries, congregations are establishing separate 501(c)(3) groups and negotiating with city officials to set up business incubators, build affordable housing, and create retirement homes for the indigent.

Meanwhile, Barbara Elliott's Center for Renewal in Houston is guiding poverty-fighters to new sources of private funding, while training them to build capacity and organizational competence. Michael Joyce, former president of the Bradley Foundation, has teamed up with Arizona business leader Paul Fleming to establish two nonprofits devoted to building support for faith-based and community charities. They need the help. James Q. Wilson points out that religious groups don't usually make the United Way list of approved charities. A United Way for Religious Outreach, established in large cities, would give new guidance to corporations and more opportunities for employees interested in supporting worthy charities.[75] If these efforts multiply and converge, large amounts of money could be redirected where it will do the most good.

Third, church and state must work together to reassert fatherhood and marriage as a national ideal. By the late 1980s, liberal columnist William Raspberry saw the handwriting on the wall: "If I could offer a single prescription for the survival of America, and particularly black America, it would be: Restore the family."[76] Former Democratic Senator Daniel Patrick Moynihan recently was asked what he considered the most significant cultural change of the last 40 years (he is old enough to know firsthand). His answer: the meltdown of the two-parent family. "The principal object of American government at every level," he says, "should be to see that children are born into intact families...and that they remain so." That cannot happen without intense suppport from churches, synagogues, mosques, and congregations of every stripe. It must be one of their principal objects as well.

You wouldn't know it from the debate of the last few months, but the most vital social function of religious communities is to strengthen families. How could it be otherwise? The task of raising children and building strong marriages demands sacrifice and moral commitments most ably taught and sustained through faith. Just consider the decline of fatherhood in America, where more than a third of all children are living apart from their biological fathers. It is no coincidence that large numbers of men have simultaneously abandoned not only their families, but any con-

75. James Q. Wilson, "Religion and Public Life: Moving Private Funds to Faith-Based Social Service Providers," in *Brookings Review*, Spring 1999, p. 41.
76. *Detroit News*, July 19, 1989, quoted in Olasky, *The Tragedy of American Compassion*, p. 202.

nection to the ethical claims of religion. As David Blankenhorn, author of *Fatherless America*, puts it, "the renewal of fatherhood in our society, if it is to occur at all, will be instigated in large measure by people of faith."[77] Whatever else congregations set themselves to do, they must not neglect what amounts to a sacred duty.

It will not be easy. In 1999, more than 1.3 million children were born to unmarried mothers, with more than two-thirds of all black children born out of wedlock.[78] Nearly half of all marriages fail, and attempts in state legislatures to toughen divorce laws have fizzled. Important institutions of government and the private sector continue to ignore efforts to promote marriage and responsible fatherhood. Says Ron Mincy, of Columbia University's School of Social Work: "Most grantmakers are very confused about the following: Should funding be in place to encourage the active involvement of fathers in the lives of children?" Only decades of muddled social policy could blur the importance of fathers to child well-being.

A Bush White House now makes it possible for government and religious institutions to mobilize around the nation's most urgent social goal: the restoration of fatherhood and marriage. Any faith-based agenda that fails to place the two-parent family at its center will founder.

The President has only begun to make the connection. Earlier this year he appeared at a National Summit on

---

77. David Blankenhorn, "The Spirit of the Fatherhood Movement," in *The Faith Factor in Fatherhood*, Don Eberly, ed. (Lanham, Md.: Lexington Books, 1999), p. xiii.
78. See *The Index of Leading Cultural Indicators 2001*.

Fatherhood in Washington, D.C., gave high praise to the fatherhood movement, and earmarked $64 million in his budget for programs that strengthen fatherhood. More importantly, he named Wade Horn, president of the National Fatherhood Initiative (NFI) and one of the movement's most respected advocates, as an assistant secretary at Health and Human Services. With responsibility for welfare, child care, child support, foster care, and adoption, Horn can push policy in a family-centered direction.

> THE TASK OF RAISING CHILDREN AND BUILDING STRONG MARRIAGES DEMANDS SACRIFICE AND MORAL COMMITMENTS MOST ABLY TAUGHT AND SUSTAINED THROUGH FAITH.

This issue desperately needs a bi-partisan, ecumenical approach. Despite the rhetoric of extremists, support for the two-parent family remains wide and deep, crossing political, racial, and economic lines. The administration should enlist organizations such as NFI, the Institute for Responsible Fatherhood, Marriage Savers, and the Alliance for Marriage—the latter being a coalition of religious leaders who disagree on most things, except the sanctity of marriage. Each of these groups taps the authority of religious communities to promote the two-parent family as a civic norm and the surest way to reverse cultural rot. "We now have 30 years of evidence and suffering," says Matt Daniels, president of the Alliance for Marriage. "We must use every lever available to promote marriage." It's time for the President and key members of his cabinet to begin talking that way.

Fourth, government must re-engage citizens in the task of caring for their neighbors. It is hard to deny that a massive welfare state has retarded the charitable efforts of the private sector. The most consequential role for the federal government now is to encourage more Americans to take on the work of caring for the needy. At his best, Bush seems to understand this. "I ask you to be citizens: citizens, not spectators…responsible citizens, building communities of service and a nation of character," he said at his inaugural. "Compassion is the work of a nation, not just a government," he warned in announcing his initiative. "It is citizens who turn mean streets into good neighborhoods." At Notre Dame he told students that the War on Poverty "turned too many citizens into bystanders, convinced that compassion had become the work of government alone."

Liberals loathe this talk. The logic of Bush's compassionate conservatism is that private organizations will not merely supplement but in some measure replace government welfare. But how? Private charity aimed at social services is about $20 billion per year, or just 5 percent of the cost of government welfare.[79] Conservatives argue that the system needs a massive overhaul; it is rife with waste, lack of accountability, and poor results. All true, but a reversal of public vs. private expenditures is inconceivable any time

---

79. Rector, "Implementing Welfare Reform and Restoring Marriage." Rector bases estimates of private charitable giving on Giving USA, a 1995 publication of the AAFRC Trust for Philanthropy.

soon. Nevertheless, it's a mistake to assume an ever-growing welfare state and a static culture of philanthropy.

> THE REAL MEASURE OF SUCCESS WILL NOT BE IN FEDERAL DOLLARS TO RELIGIOUS CHARITIES. IT WILL BE WHETHER THE PRESIDENT HELPS REVITALIZE THE IMPORTANCE OF RELIGION TO NATIONAL RENEWAL.

Serious reform will not come about by expanding federal grants to nonprofits, whether religious or secular. Instead, political leaders must commit themselves to policies that empower taxpayers, philanthropists, and the poor themselves—to support and embrace the most effective charities and character-shaping institutions. "That is a much bigger deal in the long run than anything that will happen with government," says DiIulio. "That's where the money is."[80]

Tax incentives to boost private giving are a step in the right direction. Bush proposed extending the charitable deduction to non-itemizers—about 70 percent of all taxpayers—to generate perhaps $15 billion in additional donations each year. Legislation passed in the House, however, gutted the plan. The administration wanted the initiative to match the amount of the standard deduction, about $4,300 for single returns. It was capped at $25 per person, a derisory sum. The Senate isn't likely to approve a better version without serious White House lobbying.

---

80. Fred Barnes, "In DiIulio Bush Trusts," *The Weekly Standard*, May 28, 2001, p. 15.

Another way to loosen government's grip on tax dollars helping the needy is to create a tax credit for charitable giving. Though tax credits for corporate and foundation giving may be useful, that's not where the action is. Despite the rapid growth of foundations (the number has doubled to about 47,000 over the last decade), the greatest source of philanthropic action helping the poor comes from individuals and families. Personal giving, in fact, still accounts for three-fourths of the roughly $200 billion in annual donations.[81]

By allowing every family to give a portion of what it owes in taxes to local charities—religious or secular—the state would admit it can't solve every social problem on its own. The essential thing is to reduce public spending by the value of the credit. If—as Bush proposed earlier this year—the average taxpaying family could direct $500 of its tax bill to private organizations assisting the needy, families would become much more savvy about effective charities in their own neighborhood. This could help shift responsibility for the poor from distant government bureaucracies to citizens and community-based groups.

The administration lost interest in its tax credit plan early in this year's debate, and it's been dropped from the most recent House and Senate faith-based legislation. Some worry about how to limit eligibility to groups actually fighting poverty, not lobbying for more federal money. Others don't like the idea of using tax policy to favor one kind of charity over another. Encouraging experiments at

---

81. Karen Arenson, "Charitable Giving Surged Again in '99, by an Estimated 9%," *The New York Times*, May 25, 2000.

the state level may be a wiser route to take. States such as North Carolina, Michigan, and Arizona already have enacted some form of the idea.[82]

Another crucial part of the equation is the poor themselves. The next phase of welfare reform must further strengthen individual choice and responsibility through a comprehensive voucher system. With a publicly funded certificate in hand, recipients—not government—choose the programs they think can best help them. At root is a moral argument, that those in need should have more choices—more control—over their own destiny.

Although the Supreme Court has yet to decide the constitutionality of school vouchers, proponents are winning the policy debate. Under all the faith-based legislation enacted since 1996, protections for religious groups receiving government vouchers are even stronger than those involving grants: Programs can be infused with religious teaching from top to bottom, no questions asked. For more than a decade, poor families have used publicly funded certificates to pay for daycare at church-run facilities, without any court challenges to slow them down. HUD gives billions of dollars in housing subsidies through vouchers or certificates, allowing families to decide where to live. Just before leaving office, Bill Clinton signed a bill allowing drug addicts to use federal vouchers in religious drug-treatment programs. Not all human services could or should be voucherized. But many of the most important—welfare

---

82. See Margy Walter "Charity Tax Credits: Federal Policy and Three Leading States," report published by the Annie E. Casey Foundation and the Pew Forum on Religion and Public Life, May 2001.

assistance, after-school programs, maternity homes—are ripe for a serious voucher initiative.

A voucher plan for faith-based and community charities also could gain wide political support. The legislation approved by the House (H.R. 7) allows federal grants covered under its provisions to be converted to vouchers. It would give federal administrators discretion to convert all or part of about $53 billion in existing grant programs. True, as the recent battle over Bush's education plan makes clear, opposition to school vouchers remains strong. But the dynamic of a public education establishment in league with radical separationists makes that a different debate. Conservative critics of charitable choice tend to like vouchers. Liberal opponents quietly admit they find them much more acceptable than direct grants, as long as the poor have access to needed services.

All of these ideas carry risks. But undoing the damage of the government-run compassion business will not be easy. Limiting government is half the equation; empowering citizens and the private sector is the other half. Says Mark Blitz, professor of political philosophy at Claremont McKenna College: "It is hard to see what broad effect philanthropic programs can have unless government restrains itself and allows vigorous and radical private efforts."[83]

Fifth, the President and his cabinet should deliver a series of speeches recalling America's historic alliance of faith and democratic freedom. The level of ignorance

---

83. Mark Blitz, "Philanthropy and Public Needs," in *Giving Better, Giving Smarter: Working Papers of the National Commission on Philanthropy and Civic Renewal*, p. 11.

about the essentials of the American founding has hit breathtaking depths. During last year's presidential race, for example, Senator Joe Lieberman was scolded for citing George Washington's Farewell Address to argue that religious belief is the best way to build citizens of character.[84] The *New York Times* editorialized that Lieberman "seemed to cross the boundaries of tolerance" by failing to realize that "this sort of talk is offensive to many highly ethical citizens who are not religious."[85]

What these elites find so offensive, it seems, is America's most distinctive contribution to Western democracy—freedom of religious belief as the brick and mortar of republican government. The Framers clearly believed that political liberty depends on citizens who can govern themselves, which means freedom requires virtue. Otherwise, the state intervenes to prevent social chaos, and the result is tyranny. But it takes more than laws to sustain morality. It requires religion—not the enfeebled variety of an established church, but the vibrant faith of individual believers and independent congregations, free to engage civic and political life.

---

84. In his Farewell Address, Washington linked religious belief to political stability: "Of all the dispositions and habits which lead to political prosperity, Religion and morality are indispensable supports...Whatever may be conceded to the influence of refined education on minds of peculiar structure, reason and experience both forbid us to expect that National morality can prevail in exclusion of religious principle." See Matthew Spalding and Patrick J. Garrity, *A Sacred Union of Citizens: George Washington's Farewell Address and the American Character* (Lanham, Md.: Rowman & Littlefield Publishers, Inc., 1996).
85. "Mr. Lieberman's Religious Words," *The New York Times*, August 31, 2000.

This helps explain why all of the state constitutions, in the aftermath of Independence, carved out special protections for religious freedom. It explains why, in approving the Northwest Ordinance—the most important legislative act preceding the Constitution—the Founders made the promotion of religion an indispensable part of government policy: "Religion, morality, and knowledge being necessary to good government and the happiness of mankind, schools and the means of education shall forever be encouraged."

John Adams was typical of America's early political leadership. "We have no government armed with powers capable of contending with human passions unbridled by morality and religion," he wrote. "Avarice, ambition, revenge, or gallantry would break the strongest cords of our Constitution as a whale goes through a net." Social thinker Os Guinness describes this as the "eternal triangle" of the American political order: Freedom requires virtue, virtue requires faith, and faith requires freedom. This was, more or less, the view of nearly all the Framers, even the most irreligious among them. "Few intelligent leaders today see religion as vital to liberty, or give religion a constructive place in national renewal," Guinness says. "There is quite simply no greater seachange from the world of the American Framers to the world of contemporary American intellectuals than this one."[86]

The vision and energy of the nation's religious institutions assisting the poor is the most vivid practical expression of this basic insight. Bush put it eloquently in his

---

86. Os Guinness, *The Great Experiment: Faith and Freedom in the American Republic* (Burke, Va.: The Trinity Forum, 1999), p. xi.

Independence Day message in Philadelphia: "America's founding documents give us religious liberty in principle; these Americans show us religious liberty in action." Nevertheless, if the faith-based initiative is to advance, the White House must remind all Americans—especially opinion leaders—of the nation's deep attachment to faith as the fount of social stability. Bush's plan is not, as some critics charge, the slippery slope to theocracy. But neither is it indifferent to the secularized condition of public life. The great challenge now is to forge a consensus about how to achieve and maintain a re-moralized, yet civil public square.

What counts as justice and freedom for all Americans as religious believers and government partner for the social good? The President and his team must draw on the nation's historic insights into this question and deliver them in terms all citizens—believers and nonbelievers—can understand. Areas that need special attention include education, social welfare, and law. The President's cabinet members must sound the same themes of civility, faith, and freedom. Nothing short of sustained, high-level leadership will cure opinionmakers of their historical amnesia or quiet the cranky voices of church-state militants.

FIGHTING FOR
THE GOOD SAMARITANS

*R*estoring the proper role of religion in America is intimately linked to reviving civil society. By drawing special attention to the private sector, the President is making it more difficult to ignore the redemptive influence of the faithful—men and women guided by a robust belief in God and a relentless love of neighbor. Indeed, America has been especially blessed by its communities of faith. "In the United States religion exercises but little influence upon the laws and upon the details of public opinion," wrote Alexis de Tocqueville after his 1830s visit. "But it directs the customs of the community, and, by regulating domestic life, it regulates the state."[87] Now there's a line that sends shivers up secularist spines.

Nevertheless, rigid church-state separationists must not be allowed to rewrite the nation's past—or decide its future. Americans increasingly believe that the surest road to moral and social uplift is by way of Jerusalem, not the U.S. Department of Health and Human Services. A survey conducted by the Campaign Study Group asked respondents to name the most important problem-solvers in their communities. Local police topped the list, followed by

---

87. Alexis de Tocqueville, *Democracy in America,* Vol. I (New York: Vintage Classics, 1990), p. 304.

churches, synagogues, mosques and charitable groups. The federal government was 14th, followed only by labor unions.[88] A recent Gallup Poll found that 69 percent of the respondents believe that faith-based organizations do the best job of helping youth in the community.

> AMERICANS INCREASINGLY BELIEVE THAT
> THE SUREST ROAD TO MORAL AND SOCIAL
> UPLIFT IS BY WAY OF JERUSALEM, NOT THE
> U.S. DEPARTMENT OF HEALTH AND
> HUMAN SERVICES.

At the same time, a survey by Public Agenda showed that most people think government—through the courts, schools, and statehouses—is too antagonistic to religious organizations.[89] We might have seen it coming. Fifty years ago even a secularist like Supreme Court Justice William O. Douglas worried that if church and state were always kept at arm's length, they would become pitted against each other. Instead, writing for the majority in *Zorach* v. *Clausen*, Justice Douglas saw "no constitutional requirement which makes it necessary for government to be hostile to religion and to throw its weight against efforts to widen the effective scope of religious influence."[90] Yet this is precisely the political culture we have endured for decades.

---

88. William Gibson, "Soul-Searching Over Bush's Proposal," *The Chicago Tribune*, February 9, 2001.
89. Steve Farkas, Jean Johnson, and Toly Foleno, "For Goodness' Sake: Why So Many Want Religion to Play a Greater Role in American Life," report from Public Agenda, 2001.

Will Bush's faith-based initiative successfully challenge this regime? It depends. Establishing an Office of Faith-Based and Community Initiatives was in itself the start of a remarkable effort to link religious belief to social renewal. Bush has even dubbed the office "the engine that drives the administration's goal of reorienting federal social policy across the board." That's not realistic, given the enormity of the task versus the office's small staff and limited authority. Nevertheless, the President's attack on policies that discriminate against religion puts secularists on the defensive. His appeal to minority religious leaders is helping to energize urban churches. His trust in community-based groups upsets Potomac paternalism, while his attention to their character-shaping work is a rebuke to the liberal fixation on material poverty.

More Americans seem ready to hear that rebuke than in perhaps a generation. In the immediate post-Clinton era, the opportunity is ripe not merely to inject more piety in our politics, but to reaffirm the bond between morality, religion, and democratic self-government. Until that happens, it is difficult to see how the storms of cultural decline could be stilled.

By all accounts, Americans want to make more room for faith in the public square. According to a recent poll by the Pew Forum on Religion and Public Life, a full three out of four people support the President's initiative in principle. In

---

90. Opinion of Justice William O. Douglas in *Zorach* v. *Clauson*, 343 U.S. 306 (1952), in *Religious Liberty in the Supreme Court*, Terry Eastland, ed. (Washington, D.C.: Ethics and Public Policy Center, 1993), pp. 107–109.

this, thinkers such as Jean Bethke Elshtain, professor of social and political ethics at the University of Chicago, see "a cultural moment." There is a growing recognition that American civic life is in deep trouble, and that government action cannot repair the damage. "And if there's one institution still up and running, it's going to be the church," she says. "This is a moment we couldn't have had four years ago."

Four years hence and the moment may be gone. The apologists for cultural decline will not mourn its passing. But others may wish they'd spent less time as gloomy prophets and more time fighting for the Good Samaritans. For surely it is they who bring hope to those in the darkness of addictions, who rescue the weak from life on the streets, who, as the Scriptures say, "turn the hearts of the fathers back to their children."

JOSEPH LOCONTE is the William E. Simon Fellow in Religion and a Free Society at the Heritage Foundation. He is a commentator on religion and culture for National Public Radio's "All Things Considered" and the author of *Seducing the Samaritan: How Government Contracts Are Reshaping Social Services.*

The Heritage Foundation

The Heritage Foundation is committed to building an America where freedom, opportunity, prosperity and civil society flourish

FOUNDED IN 1973, The Heritage Foundation is a research and educational institute—a think tank—whose mission is to formulate and promote conservative public policies based on the principles of free enterprise, limited government, individual freedom, traditional American values, and a strong national defense.

Heritage's staff pursues this mission by performing timely, accurate research on key policy issues and effectively marketing these findings to our primary audiences: members of Congress, key congressional staff members, policymakers in the executive branch, the nation's news media, and the academic and policy communities. Heritage's products include publications, articles, lectures, conferences, and meetings.

Governed by an independent Board of Trustees, The Heritage Foundation is a nonpartisan, tax-exempt institution. Heritage relies on the private financial support of the general public—individuals, foundations, and corporations—for its income, and accepts no government funds and performs no contract work. Heritage is one of the nation's largest public policy research organizations. More than 200,000 contributors make it the most broadly supported think tank in America.

For more information, or to support our work, please contact The Heritage Foundation at (800) 544-4843 or visit *www.heritage.org*.